Easy Step by Step Guide

To

Marketing

By

Pauline Rowson

ROWMARK

Published by Rowmark Publishing Limited
65 Rogers Mead
Hayling Island
Hampshire
PO11 0PL
UK

ISBN 0 9532987 6 0

First printed 1999
Re printed and revised 1999

Printed in Great Britain

Note: The material contained in this book is set out in good faith for general
guidance and no liability can be accepted for loss or expense incurred as a result of
relying in particular circumstances on statements made in this book.

eBook edition distributed by:
Summersdale Publishers Ltd
46 West Street
Chichester
West Sussex
PO19 1RP
UK
www.summersdale.com

About the author

Pauline Rowson is a Marketing, Publicity and Training Consultant who runs her own business, Pauline Rowson Marketing Services and Training. She is qualified in marketing and is a member of the Chartered Institute of Marketing. She regularly advises businesses on all aspects of their marketing and sales. Her clients are drawn from many sectors including the professions, engineering, manufacturing, farming, education, service and charitable organisations.

In addition she runs training courses in marketing, sales, management and personal development.

In her spare time she is a writer of crime and historical fiction.

CONTENTS

Chapter Five
Pricing

Chapter Six
The Market Place and Marketing Planning 74

Chapter Seven
The Marketing Action Plan 84

Other Easy Step by Step Guides in the series include:

The Easy Step By Step Guide to Telemarketing, Cold Calling & Appointment Making - £9.99

The Easy Step By Step Guide to Selling - £9.99

The Easy Step by Step Guide to Stress & Time Management - £9.99

All the above guides are available on order from all good booksellers and direct from:

Rowmark Limited
65 Rogers Mead
Hayling Island
Hampshire
PO11 0PL
Telephone: 023 9246 1931
Fax: 023 9246 0574
E mail: enquiries@rowmark.co.uk

Or via our web site www.rowmark.co.uk

Introduction

All businesses have one thing in common: they need customers. Without customers quite simply there is no business. Rather obvious you might be thinking but it's amazing how many people forget this time and time again.

So how do you get customers? How do you get them to buy from you - and not just once but again and again? How do you build a competitive edge for your business? How do you develop new products and services and stay ahead of the competition? All these and many more are the challenges for a business.

This book will look at these challenges and help you to meet them. It will help you to understand the basic meaning of marketing and take you through a series of steps so that you can make your marketing work for you. There is no jargon and there are no trendy theories, simply tips on how to do it! I hope you enjoy reading it.

How to use this guide

This guide is written in as clear a style as possible to aid you. I recommend that you read it through from beginning to end and then dip into it to refresh your memory. The boxes in each chapter contain tips to help you and at the end of each chapter are some action points for you to relate to your own business. Also at the end of each chapter is a handy summary of the points covered.

Chapter one

What is successful marketing?

What you will learn from this guide

This guide looks at how you can market your business more effectively. It will provide you with a greater understanding of what is meant by marketing and, I hope, will help strip away the mystique so that you may win more customers and keep those customers coming back for more.

This guide will show you:

- ❍ how to understand your customers and their needs
- ❍ how to make your organisation more marketing orientated
- ❍ how to use some of the promotional tools to target your customers and potential customers
- ❍ how to build a competitive edge for your organisation
- ❍ how to draw up a marketing plan for your business by following the steps in this guide.

So what is marketing?

Successful marketing is about knowing your customers and communicating with them in the most effective way in order to win more business from them. It is about understanding who your customers are and anticipating what they want, not just today or tomorrow, but next year, the year after, and so on.

Successful marketing is about having a business that is flexible enough to respond quickly to changing demands. And a workforce that is willing to co-operate with your customers, not treat them as if they were public enemy number one!

Successful marketing is not something that you can pick up today and get results from tomorrow. It is not something that you do ad hoc, or when the mood takes you. It does not mean simply placing an advertisement in a newspaper or magazine and then waiting for the telephone to ring and orders to flood in, because it just doesn't happen that way.

But neither is **successful marketing** any great mystery or rocket science. Much of it is basic common sense with an added touch of creativity. That creativity is the ability to open your mind and to put yourself in your customer's shoes.

Successful marketing means putting the customer at the heart of your business so that everything you do is driven by that philosophy.

The definition from the **Chartered Institute of Marketing** summarises all the above points very well.

> **'Marketing is the management process responsible for identifying, anticipating and satisfying customer requirements profitably.'**
> *Chartered Institute of Marketing*

This may sound like a tall order but if you take a planned approach to your marketing it isn't. I am going to show you how to do this. I will take you through the stages, step by step, and show you how to achieve a marketing orientated organisation that will win you more business and keep your customers coming back for more.

So let's start by seeing just how marketing friendly your organisation is. Take a look at the questions listed below and see how your organisation rates.

How marketing orientated is your business?

Can you tick yes to all of these questions?

❑ **Are your services or products created with the customer in mind?**

This means producing what your customers want and not what you think they want, or what you like producing. You may be very good at making widgets. You may want to fill your whole life with making widgets but it's not a bit of good if no one wants to buy them.

The question is not as simple either as it first appears because customers' needs and wants change, technology advances, fashions alter. Companies may spend thousands researching and developing products only to find that they are too late.

❑ **Do you track your customers' attitudes and behaviour?**

This means being constantly in touch with your customers. How often do you talk to them? How often do you survey them? Do you know what your customers buy, how they buy and when? Do you know what they want from you?

❑ **Is your organisation organised and co-ordinated in the service of your customers?**

This means that, not only do you have to give the customer what he or she wants, but that you also have to deliver it in the way he or she wants. If your customers wish to be invoiced monthly do you invoice them monthly? If they wish to buy direct through mail order or the Internet do you provide that service for them?

❑ **Are you and your staff customer friendly and responsive?**

If you've ever heard any of your staff say the following then you shouldn't have ticked this box.

○ " We've being doing it this way for the last twenty years" (which, of course, means they can't possibly change).

○ " Well you must appreciate that we have our administration to think about."

○ " It's more costly for us to do it that way."

And so on and so on…excuses, excuses…

Perhaps you are too busy to stop and think about the way you are doing things, but if you don't make time to do this, then you could be missing out on valuable opportunities. Finding new ways of supplying and servicing your customers is what will give you a competitive edge. What was acceptable ten, five or even two years ago may not be acceptable today and will certainly change tomorrow.

❑ **Are your staff motivated and all pulling in the same direction?**

Do you know where your business is heading? And if so does your staff know? If they don't, then how can you expect them to help you achieve your aims? You need your staff working for you and not against you.

❑ **Does the same vision and identity exist both inside and outside the organisation?**

Do you know what your organisation stands for in the market place? How do your customers see it? How would you like it to be seen? What words describe its personality? Here are some words that might be used to describe an organisation's personality:

○ professional

○ friendly

○ helpful

○ hi-tech.

Once having defined the personality of your company, ask yourself if this personality is communicated both within the company and outside it. Is the same message being communicated? If not, then conflict and confusion will arise and you will be wasting effort, not to mention money, and you will lose potential business.

❑ Do you consistently deliver your promises?

Organisations that consistently deliver what they promise will gain a competitive advantage. But too many companies don't deliver. And they fail to deliver, again and again. Sometimes through over promising and sometimes through gross inefficiencies. If this is happening in your company then all the money you spend trying to win new business might just as well be poured down the drain. There is no point in having worked hard to win customers if you lose them through failing to deliver what they want.

❑ Are you in business to make a profit?

The answer to this is fairly obvious. Even non profit making organisations have to balance budgets and make them stretch ever further these days. Charities need revenue and to make every donation count, and schools need to make their budgets stretch to almost impossible lengths. So you need to make every penny spent on your marketing count.

❑ Do you innovate enough?

How often do you look at producing new services or products for your customers or at new ways of doing things? Again, the organisation that innovates is the one that is going to build and maintain a competitive edge.

So how did you score?

Were you able to tick all the above points? If so, well done. But as you know, and I have already mentioned, it is not enough to be able to tick them once. If you wish to build and maintain your competitive edge then you have to keep asking these questions and keep providing the right answers to them.

Throughout this book you will, I hope, learn how to make your organisation more marketing orientated.

Action Points

1. Take a look at your organisation and the services or products it produces - are these what the customer wants?

2. Have you asked your customers what they want? Do you tap into your customers' comments about your products or services? Start now - telephone a sample of customers, or devise a questionnaire to capture their comments after a transaction.

3. Gain feedback from your staff if they regularly interface with your customers.

In summary

○ Marketing is a long-term strategy not a short term one

○ Marketing is a management philosophy that should run right through your business

○ Marketing means getting to know your customers and thinking like them

○ Marketing is giving your customers what they want, when they want it, how they want it and delivering it in a profitable way

○ Marketing is anticipating what your customers will want in the future and ensuring you deliver this

○ Your services/products must be created with the customer in mind

○ Your organisation must be organised and co-ordinated in the service of your customers

○ Your staff must be motivated and all pulling in the same direction

○ The same vision and identity must exist both inside and outside the organisation

○ You must consistently deliver your promises

○ You need to constantly innovate.

Chapter two

Know who your customers are

The more you know about your target customers the more successful you will be. This is because you will be able to communicate with them more effectively. Let me explain. People need to be shown the benefits of why they should buy from you and those benefits have to be communicated to them in a language they can relate to. You can't do this until you know who your customers are and understand them.

> **You have to put yourself in your customers' shoes and think like your customers.**

This isn't always as easy as it sounds. Your customers may be a different age or gender to you. They may have a very different lifestyle. They may range across many diverse industries. Whoever they are it is your task to understand them and communicate with them. Whatever your own beliefs and values you have to suspend these and think like your target customers.

Of course, you can read all the market research carried out on your customers - and you should. You can apply the common sense, scientific approach of marketing - but you will also need an open mind and imagination to make the further leap - the creative element of marketing. So how do you do this?

> **You need to get to know your customers.**

Understanding your customers

In order to understand your customers it is easier if you can divide them into identifiable groups with similar characteristics. This way you can also target them more effectively. By understanding them and targeting them you can sell more to them and you can stop throwing money away chasing customers who you can't sell to, who are unprofitable, or who are unlikely to buy from you.

Dividing your customers into groups

If you are already running a business the best place to start is by analysing your customer base to see what type of people or businesses currently buy from you. New businesses should have a clear idea of their target markets from the beginning.

You can begin by dividing your customers into two distinct groups:

○ **business customers**

○ **consumers.**

Some of you may be operating in both markets, some only in the one. From these two groups you can then subdivide your customers further.

For example, if you are in the business-to-business market i.e. you sell to businesses then you can subdivide your customers by the following categories:

O   type of business

O   size of business

O   geographical location

O   position of purchaser.

If you are in consumer markets then you can subdivide your customers by the following categories:

O   by the gender of the customer

O   by age

O   by geographical location - you may even know the type of house they live in

O   Are they single/married or co-habiting?

O   What is their lifestyle - what sort of hobbies do they have, what sort of magazines and newspapers do they read?

O   Have they children and if so what is their age range?

O   Are they working, unemployed, retired?

O   What is their economic background and status?

Let's now take a look at this in more detail.

Business Customers

1. By Business type or Standard Industry Classification.

What type of business are your customers in? For example, are they in the construction industry, computing, engineering or retail etc.? You may have customers in a diverse range of industries. Give each industry sector a code so that you can pull lists of them off your database. You can then analyse these customer sectors to see what they are buying from you, how much and when. You will also be able to target them more effectively. You can divide your customers by using the Government's Standard Industry Classification. You can obtain a list from your local Chamber of Commerce or in the reference section of a library.

2. By size of the company.

Are your customers from large companies, medium or small companies? Or are they from a range of these? There are many ways you can define size:

○ by turnover

○ by the number of outlets or branches

○ by the number of employees.

The buying process in a large company will be very different from a small company. It may take you longer to break into larger companies. You may have to go through several people until you reach the decision maker, whereas in the smaller business, you may get the Managing Director answering the telephone to you.

> **Different companies will have different needs;
> they will speak different languages.**

You will be targeting different people. You need to understand this and tailor your message and your marketing material to suit your audience. This way you will have greater success.

3. By geographical area.

Where are your customers based? Which areas? Are they local, national, overseas? How do you reach them? How does this affect your marketing and pricing?

You may have other categories to help you identify who your customers are.

An Example

Take for example a four star hotel situated just off a motorway. It has easy access and lots of parking. It has a gym and swimming pool. It has conference facilities and meeting rooms that it would like to fill, either for one day events, or for two/three/four day conferences when the bedrooms could also be utilised. Who would it target through its marketing? The facilities aren't likely to be the cheapest.

The hotel is therefore better off targeting the larger companies; those who perhaps have a sales force or a large number of employees, those who hold product launches. Or it could target the Professional sector which markets through seminars, or training organisations that would hold one or two day courses. It could also target national organisations like Institutes and Associations who hold annual conferences. It can therefore begin to define both the sectors it would like to target, and the size of the organisation most likely to buy its services.

The hotel is least likely to spend its time and money targeting the small business, the sole proprietor type business and those with few staff.

It can also define the geographical area it is targeting: local businesses over a certain size with a certain number of employees. And it can target further afield, the UK in total perhaps.

So you can see from this that we can define our target audience. Having defined them we can find out how to reach them, through direct marketing to them, or advertising in the magazines they are most likely to read. We can direct our money and efforts into communicating the benefits of our hotel and conference centre to them and so get them to use us. We are not wasting time and money chasing business that is least likely to use us.

Now let's take a closer look at consumer markets.

Consumer Markets

The area of consumer marketing is very sophisticated. Some companies spend vast amounts of money in understanding just exactly who their customers are.

Information on the breakdown of the population is provided through the census. This information is taken by companies and agencies and cross referenced with other information gathered through surveys, research etc. to provide organisations with a breakdown of consumers; their buying habits, where they live, their occupation, leisure interests, age, social status and so on. The loyalty cards issued by many large stores are just another means of capturing information about the buying habits and breakdown of customers.

The socio-economic model of dividing the population into distinct groups has been with us a long time, since 1911 in fact, when Britain's working structure looked very different. Then it was possible to label people as manual/non manual, or skilled/unskilled. Since then, manufacturing industry has declined and the service sector has grown. Today you can no longer measure just skill, which is why a new classification is to be introduced in 2001 when the government conducts the next nation-wide census.

I have provided a breakdown of this new classification. It is based on occupation and has seven major classes:

1. Higher managerial and professional occupations
      1.1 Employers and managers in larger organisations
      1.2 Higher professionals
2. Lower managerial and professional occupations
3. Intermediate occupations
4. Small employers and own account workers
5. Lower supervisory, craft and related occupations
6. Semi routine occupations
7. Routine occupations.

An additional category to cover those who have never had paid employment and the long-term unemployed will be added. You can also divide your customers into the following categories and add these factors to the above model.

2. By type of house.

Are your target customers more likely to live in a large, detached modern house or a terraced house in an inner city? Do they live in council houses or in cottages in the country? And what sort of area of the country do they live in? Is it town, suburb, countryside or a mixture of these?

3. By lifestyle.

What is their lifestyle? What hobbies do they enjoy? Do they go out to eat and if so where? Where do they shop and what sort of goods do they buy? Do they take holidays abroad and if so what kind of holiday? What newspapers and magazines do they read?

4. By lifecycle.

By this I mean are they married or single? Do they live together? Do they have children and if so what are the ages of the children. This will influence what is bought. Are they retired and if so how affluent?

You can also divide your customers by:

O   age

O   gender

O   ethnic origin.

Therefore, by looking at the above categories you may be in a better position to understand what markets you are in and who you should be targeting. Obviously whom you are targeting will dictate to a certain degree, the price, distribution, availability of the product or service, its name and branding. More about this in later chapters.

Once you have defined whom you are targeting - i.e. who is most likely to buy your products/services- you can obtain lists of names and addresses from the companies who rent or sell this information.

Our Four Star Hotel

If we return to our four star hotel then, using the above consumer categories, we can define who is most likely to stay in the hotel. We can say what their background is likely to be, their ages, where they live and what type of house they live in. We can define their most likely lifestyle and, having done this, we can then place our advertising in the magazines they are most likely to read. Or we could rent or buy a list of names and target them through direct marketing.

So again you can see that we want to direct our money and energy into targeting people who are most likely to buy from us.

But what if I can sell to everybody?

Some business owners tell me they can sell to 'everybody.' And, of course they may be able to sell to 'everybody.' If someone turns up on our hotel doorstep for example wanting to stay overnight, or to hire a room for a conference, we're not going to send them away but that is very different from targeting them.

You can **sell** your products or services to whoever is prepared to pay for them. But when it comes to **marketing**, how do you market your products or services to 'everybody.' How do you reach 'everybody?' Also if you target 'everybody' what message do you use? It would have to appeal to a very wide range of people with diverse interests and backgrounds. Sometimes your marketing message will hit the right note with the right people, the rest of the time it will be wasted and so will your money.

You need to make your marketing work, so don't waste time and money chasing customers who are unlikely to buy from you, or who are unprofitable. Know what markets you are in and understand those markets thoroughly. It will pay dividends for you.

By analysing your customer groups clearly you can begin to answer the questions:

Where are my customers?
How do I reach them?
How do I communicate with them?

When you look at your target groups of customers you will probably find that some groups are easier to reach than others. Some will also be more profitable, or better payers. It is these you want to concentrate on.

Once having decided *whom* to target, you can then decide *how* to target them. How do you reach them? Where can you advertise for example? What other promotional tools would they respond to? In addition, what sort of message would appeal to them and what kind of image? More about this in later chapters but if you don't undertake this first basic exercise then you could be advertising, or sending direct mail to the wrong people - a waste of time and money.

In my experience, many businesses skip this first stage and end up throwing money down the drain because they simply do not understand what market they are in. They try to be all things to all people which simply doesn't work.

Questions to ask about each group of customers

Once you have carried out the above exercise you will need to ask the following questions:

○ How large is that group of customers?

○ Where are they and how easy is it for me to reach them?

○ How many competitors are there in the market place in relation to that group?

○ How can what I am offering be significantly different to my competitors?

○ How easy is it to enter or win new business from this group?

○ How costly is it to enter or win business from this group of customers?

The answers to the above questions will help you decide where you should be spending both your money and time on marketing. You need to reach the people you think are most likely to buy from you. You may also need to adopt different marketing tactics for different groups of customers. Above all don't forget your existing customers. Could you be selling more to them? Your existing customers are the easiest group of people to sell to, yet many businesses overlook them. You should be keeping your name in front of them on a regular basis, perhaps through a newsletter. You should be informing them of new products/services. You should be telephoning them regularly. You should be up selling or cross selling other services or products to them.

The difference between consumer buying and business buying

Let me finally touch upon the differences between consumer buying and business buying. The obvious one is that consumers buy for their own personal use whilst businesses buy for their organisation's use.

Generally speaking in a business there are more people involved in the buying decision. You could find that the person who uses the equipment, as well as the person who places the order, and the person who signs the cheque could all influence the buying decision.

Organisations can impose buying policies and the purchasing decision usually generates lots of paperwork. Decisions will also be made on what that organisation needs as opposed to what it wants.

The need to buy in an organisation can take into account the objectives of the company, the policies and procedures. The profit motive may be a strong factor in reaching a purchasing decision. However, not all decisions to buy are based on these objective reasons but often subjective reasons come into play. The decision to purchase may also be made based on the relationship you have with the decision maker and whether or not he or she likes you!

In some organisations there are professional buyers. These are expert in analysing the needs of the company and whether or not the product or service bought match these needs.

Reciprocal buying arrangements may also mean that firms buy from firms that buy from them and supplier loyalty may be involved.

A greater flexibility is often needed in financial arrangements. This could involve options to lease, rent, or give an extension of credit, or provide buy back arrangements.

Many industrial products are expensive to develop and manufacture, as well as being expensive to purchase, so it could mean that the buying cycle is longer. Industrial buyers of capital equipment may take a few years to make a decision to buy from you and this can be the same in professional markets where the decision to change accountants or lawyers could take many years.

Many organisations will seek tenders by buyers for goods and services and contracts may be drawn up for long-term supply arrangements rather than for one off purchases.

Your Database

It is essential to capture information about your customers on a database. A database is a vital marketing and management information tool for driving your business forward. You should record existing customers and their transactions.

You should also use the database to review past customers. If someone has bought once and then stopped buying from you, find out why and get them back. If you have done something to upset them then you want to know about it. You can only put things right if you listen to them and accept their comments. And then, of course, act on them.

You should also have a prospect database made up of individuals or businesses that could, with regular targeting, become customers.

Database Advantages

A database will help you:

O   Track developments in your customer base

O   Identify prospects and their potential to buy

O   Target key customers and prospects with the right messages

O   Monitor the success or otherwise of your marketing activity

O   Identify areas of improvements i.e. customer care: what problems and complaints are you regularly receiving?

O   Monitor sales and decline of sales of products/services.

If you don't have a database, or use it properly, all your forecasts will be based on highly suspect, historical data.

Your database should contain:

O   Details about the decision making process of your customers i.e. who buys and their position. This is particularly relevant in business markets.

O   What the customer has bought in the last couple of years.

O   Where the customer has come from. You may be receiving enquiries from your Web Site. If you are then make sure your Web Site has a database function and can transfer names and addresses captured on line that can then be mail merged with a word document. The customer, or prospect, can then be communicated with ease and on a regular basis. On line buying sites should have this function as a matter of course.

O   You may also like to ensure that your Web Site holds a customer survey asking the browser where he or she heard of you and what prompted them to look at your site, or purchase from it. This information can then be analysed and any pattern of buying identified. It will also help you to monitor the effectiveness of your marketing activity.

O   What the value and volume of sales per customer is.

O   If a representative visits customers, or a telemarketing person calls them, make sure the date and result of the call, or the visit, is logged and the date of the next call is flagged up.

O   A brief history of the customer.

○ A breakdown of your customers and prospects by industry type, geographical area, number of employees etc. or consumer type and background information.

○ A list of prospects and details on them.

○ The mailing history.

○ The marketing history.

> **Organisations need to ask what is being bought - by whom, when, how often and why are they buying?**

Action Points

1. Look at your own customer base and analyse who is buying from you.

○ What sort of consumers or businesses?

○ Where do they come from?

○ How much do they spend?

○ Which are the most profitable sectors?

○ Identify which sectors or groups of customers you are going to target?

2. Start capturing information about your customers on a database and analyse it on a regular basis.

In summary

○ You will need to identify who your customers are. Break your customers down into easily identifiable groups with similar characteristics.

○ Business customers can be broken down into:
    industry type
    size
    geographical areas.

○ Consumers can be broken down into:
    socio-economic groupings
    type of house
    geographical area
    lifestyle
    lifecycle
    age
    gender
    ethnic origin.

○ Then look at what each group of customers buy, how much and when.

○ Look at the groups of customers in relation to your market place - how large is the group?

○ What geographical area does it cover? Is this easily accessible to you?

○ How profitable is the group of customers?

○ How easy is it to enter or win new business from this group of customers?

❍ Don't forget your existing customers. Could you be selling more to them? Keep in regular touch with them and try to up sell and cross sell other products and services to them.

❍ Don't forget dormant or past customers. Find out why they stopped buying from you and try and win them back.

❍ There is a difference between organisational buying and consumer buying. Organisations can take longer to reach a purchasing decision and more people can be involved in the decision to purchase.

❍ Make sure you have a database to capture information on existing customers, past customers and prospects.

Chapter three

Know what your customers are buying

Having identified who your customers are you now need to identify what they are buying. Knowing this will help you to send the right message to them.

When people buy something they ask, 'Why should I? What's in it for me?' They are seeking certain benefits from buying a particular service or product. It is these benefits that you have to communicate strongly in your marketing literature in order to persuade your customers to buy from you.

Benefits and Features

> **People buy the benefits of a product
> or service not the features.**

In my experience many businesses fail to realize this which means that their literature is often written in the language of features and not benefits. Features alone do not persuade people to part with their money, or their time. Features alone will not increase sales. What will increase sales is if you can demonstrate to your potential customers the benefits of those features you are offering.

So how do you do this? You need to look at the products or services you are offering and identify for each of these the features and benefits. If you can't see a benefit how do you expect your potential customers to see it!

Here are some examples.

1. A Feature
We have a wide range of products/services.

Which means

The Benefit
We have something to suit all tastes. There is no need to shop around. We can save you time and money.

2. A Feature
We are centrally located.

Which means

The Benefit
We are easy to get to thus saving you time and hassle.

3. A Feature
We are a well established company.

Which means

The Benefit
We can give you the reassurance that we know what we're doing. We're not here today, gone tomorrow. We have the experience and expertise to give you the best advice.

4. A Feature
You can buy direct and order through our 7 day a week hotline.

Which means

The Benefit

It's cheaper, quicker and more convenient for you.

5. A Feature

We can deliver to your door.

Which means

The Benefit

There is no need to struggle into town and park. It's quicker and easier to buy from us and will save you time.

If we look back to our previous example of the hotel then one of the features I mentioned is the swimming pool. The benefit of providing this feature to delegates attending an overnight conference, or guests staying in the hotel, is that, after a hard days work or shopping, they can relax and unwind with a swim in the pool. You can tailor your message, i.e. the benefits, to suit the target audience.

Do you get the idea?

> **The two magic words that turn a feature into a benefit are *which means*.**

Perhaps you don't know what benefits your customers are buying or why they buy from you. If you don't, then you will need to ask them. It's a good idea to ask them anyway because you can take their comments and put them in your literature. The benefits they gained from buying the product/ service will appeal to other customers.

In addition, by asking your customers and prospective customers what benefits they want, you could get ideas on how to improve your services or products. You may find you need to make changes.

> **When you are reviewing what your customers are buying and why they buy, you need to ask if you are providing the right products and services in the best way.**

Developing products and services that your customers want Organisations constantly need to be looking at providing better, newer, different and more profitable products, or examining better ways of supplying customers.

Nothing stays the same. Not in life, and not in the business world. The demand for your products or services will change over a period of time and the challenge is to make sure that you monitor that change and keep adapting or developing new products and services to meet your customers' changing needs. To understand this I need to explore the concept of something called the **Product Life Cycle**.

> **The Product Life Cycle means that products go through certain phases: introduction, growth, maturity and decline.**

The Product Life Cycle states that products or services are:

O   **introduced** into the market

O   they **grow**

O   they **mature**

O   they **decline.**

Most companies have a range of products or services each of which may be in a different stage of its life cycle. However, not all products follow this life cycle. Indeed, some products have been around for a very long time and have not gone into decline. Other products have flopped at the introduction stage.

For example, products that have not declined are: Mars Bars, Heinz Baked Beans and Levi Jeans to name but a few, although Levi Jeans are currently looking at ways to keep their product alive in a changing and fickle fashion market.

Mars have extended their product life cycle by reintroducing the Mars Bar in a number of different forms. There has been king size, party pack size, miniature size, egg shaped, filled with ice cream, dark chocolate.

Levi Jeans were originally worn by cowboys in the mid west of America. They were restyled, relaunched and extended into a completely new and very different market i.e. the youth market. Again the challenge is on for them to relaunch and extend yet again as the youth market fashion trends change.

Conversely, some products never reach the growth phase but fail on introduction. Clive Sinclair's C5 for example.

And then, of course, there is the stage before introduction - product development. Many products will never see the introduction phase. Whilst others will go on to become mature products.

The key to success and continuing success lies in a company having a number of products or services at the different stages of its life cycle. Depending on what stage your product or service is at will also determine the marketing strategy, investment costs and profitability.

Let's take a look at this in more detail.

Product Development

○   There is no return on your investment

○   You have a heavy investment both in terms of time and money.

Introduction (the start of the lifecycle)

○   Your sales are low

○   Your cash flow is negative

○   Your profits are negligible

○   You are searching out new customers

○   Your Investment costs are high/marketing costs high.

Growth

○   Your sales are growing fast

○   Your profits are at peak levels

○   Your customers are growing

○   Your marketing costs are moderate to high.

Maturity

O   Your sales are starting to slow before going into decline

O   Your profits are declining

O   Your marketing costs could be high as you struggle to keep your products in front of your customers to boost sales.

Decline

O   Your sales are declining

O   Your profits are declining

O   Your cash flow levels are low

O   Customers are fewer.

When a product or service is in the growth phase its sales will be high and investment costs lower. Profit should then be reinvested into new product or service development so that when a product reaches maturity and declines there are other products and services coming along behind it to stimulate sales.

Extending the life cycle of your products or services

You can extend the product lifecycle and halt decline by **adapting your product/service.**

This means taking an existing product/service and adapting it for an existing market, or for selling it into a completely new market.

Adapting can include:

○   modifying or improving the product itself

○   improving or changing the quality

○   changing the packaging

○   changing the name

○   relaunching it

○   targeting a completely new market or new geographical area, country even

○   offering a sales incentive to buy.

If sales are declining you may decide to withdraw the product or service. You can decide whether or not to increase the price dramatically before ditching it, or you could sell it on. You may adopt certain sales promotion tactics, like offering 10% off, or 10% extra, but, of course, this will have an impact on your profitability.

Developing new products/services

Product differentiation has become a key competitive strategy and new product development an essential activity. You will need to be on the constant look out for new products or services. So where can you get ideas from? **Ideas can come from:**

O **Talking and listening to your staff**

Your staff may have more contact with the customer than you. You need to encourage your staff to ask the customer questions about the level of satisfaction experienced. Staff should then feedback those comments to you. Of course, it goes without saying that you should take those comments on board and action them if possible.

Your staff may have a wealth of ideas but they need to be encouraged to air them. You need to create a climate where ideas can be raised and welcomed, not shot down in flames. And new staff in particular should be encouraged to come forward with ideas and ways of improving things. They come into the business with a fresh pair of eyes and often ask questions as to why you are doing something in the way you are. When no one listens to them they stop asking questions and just carry on the same as everyone else - what a waste.

O **Talking and listening to your customers**

You can carry out formal research amongst your customers, asking them for their views and opinions. Or the research can be informal. Simply by asking customers what they think about your products or services can be enough. Don't forget to listen to their comments and act on them. Customer evaluation forms can also capture information and ideas.

O **From your competitors**

Firstly, know who your competitors are in each of your markets and product or service areas. You may have many competitors in different sectors and price ranges. Collect information on them. What are their strengths and weaknesses and how does this compare with your own? Can you take some of their ideas and refine them, do them better or different.

O   From published research

Take time to read trade or professional papers and magazines. There is a wealth of published information available covering a wide range of subjects. This can include information from:

O   Chambers of Commerce

O   Business Links

O   Government Statistical Services

O   Organisations, trade associations etc..

Much of the information is free so take advantage of it. It could give you new and very profitable ideas.

O   From the media

Both national and local media can provide you with information on trends. Articles can help stimulate ideas.

O   Network

Get out and about and talk to people. Attend exhibitions and seminars. Keep your eyes and ears open. But most importantly keep your mind open.

Action Points

1. Draw up a list of features and benefits for your business. Answer the customer's question,' Why should I buy from you rather than your competitor?'

2. Now look at what you are providing. Draw up a list of features and benefits for each product/ service you provide.

3. If you don't know what your customers are buying or why they buy, then find some customers and ask them.

4. Take a look at your own products/services. What is the volume of sales generated for each product/service?

5. Compare this with previous years' performance then plot your range of products or services on a life cycle. Which products would you say are in the maturity or growth phase of the Product Life Cycle? Which in decline?

6. What new products or services are being developed or introduced?

In summary

O   When people buy they ask, 'Why should I?' 'What's in it for me?' The product or service benefits must come out strongly on your marketing literature.

O   To turn a feature into a benefit add the words *which means* between them.

O   The need to constantly develop new products and services to suit your existing customers, or for new customers, is great.

O   You need to be looking at providing better, newer, different and more profitable products or ways of supplying your customers. To understand this look at where your products are on the **Product Life Cycle**.

O   The Product Life Cycle explores the concept that products go through certain phases: introduction, growth, maturity and decline.

O   Most companies have a range of products each of which may be in a different stage of its life cycle.

O   Depending on what stage your product or service is in will also determine the marketing strategy, investment costs and profitability.

O   When a product or service is in the growth phase its sales will be high and investment costs lower. Profit should then be reinvested into new product or service development.

○ You can extend the lifecycle and halt decline by **adapting the product.** This means taking an existing product or service and adapting it for an existing market, or for a completely new market.

○ If sales are declining you may decide to withdraw the product.

○ Ideas for new products or services can come from talking and listening to your staff, talking and listening to your customers. From your competitors, published research and the media.

○ Ask yourself if you are providing the right products and services to your customers in the best way.

Chapter four

Developing a Competitive Edge

One of the biggest challenges for businesses today is how to build and maintain a competitive edge. There are a number of ways of doing this, all of which are very easy to say (or write) but none of which are simple to carry out. In this chapter we look at some of the ways you may be able to build a competitive edge for your business. This could be through:

○ branding

○ image

○ price

○ product or service differentiation

○ building and maintaining an excellent reputation for providing a good service or product.

Or you could build a competitive edge for your products or services through a combination of the above. Let's examine these in greater detail.

Why Brand?

What matters is not merely what people know about your

product but how they feel about it and how it relates to their own personality and life style. People tend to buy what they are familiar with. They like to know what the product or service stands for and whether or not it is the right one for them. Branding helps them to make this choice.

> **Branding is used to define identity
> and helps people relate to the product.**

Branding is used very strongly in the fast moving consumer goods market where customer loyalty needs to be constantly fought for. But it can also be used on other products including industrial products. In the service sector and in business to business markets, image, as an aspect of branding, is very important and we will look at image in more detail later.

Branding will give a product identity and make it more easily recognisable. If people know what a brand stands for, and where it fits with their own needs, then it is easier for them to buy it.

People will ask:

O   Does this brand fit my lifestyle?

O   Does it express my identity?

O   Is it value for money?

O   How available is it?

O   What do I think about it - do I like or dislike it?

Building a Brand

Various factors go into making up a brand. These include:

O   the product itself

O   the packaging

O   the advertising

O   the brand name

O   the price

O   how and where it is distributed

O   its availability

O   its logo, colours, style, any strap lines

O   the consistency of communicating all the above which go into forming a corporate image or identity.

Branding also goes beyond this. Things like quality, service, reliability, innovation and integrity all come into play. Branding is the result of a successful marketing and business strategy. It will reflect how you train your staff in the company's values and how you manage your relationships with your customers.

Choosing a brand name

This can be a very tricky area and marketing history is littered with expensive errors. Essentially the brand name should:

O   never contradict the essential product qualities

O   not have unfortunate connotations

O   be easy to say, pronounce, catchy

O   fit onto the packaging.

Take a look at some well-known brands and companies - if I ask you to sum up what you think about them, you are summing up the brand or company personality.

O   Guinness

O   Ford

O   Mercedes

O   Waitrose

O   Tesco

O   Microsoft

O   Kellogg's Cornflakes

O   Virgin.

What words do you associate with these brands or companies?

Get someone else in your company to do the same exercise and see if you both come up with the same, or similar brand images. If you do then these companies are successfully communicating their brand image and values.

Image

Building and maintaining a favourable image of your organisation in the minds and eyes of your customers is vital. The image of the company is an essential ingredient in the choice of services and often in the choice of products. But this image has to be managed. It doesn't just happen.

So what elements go into communicating an image and how can you manage this?

All visitors to your company carry away with them an impression. You need to make sure it is the right impression.

Whether it is on the telephone or face-to-face first impressions count. Remember the saying - *You never get a second chance to make a first impression.*

People will judge not only **you** by first impressions but also **your organisation.** If the hotel used in our example earlier has dirty curtains and peeling paintwork, or the receptionist is unhelpful, then the first impressions of it won't be very good at all. I certainly wouldn't stay there and you may not either. Not only that but I would also tell others not to go there.

If a restaurant's toilets are dirty - then what are the kitchens like? I have walked out of a restaurant after seeing the state of the toilets. And I'm not the only one to do so.

How does your company treat visitors - any visitors and not just potential customers but the person who comes to clean the windows or service the photocopier, the delivery drivers and suppliers? Remember they all carry away with them an impression of your company. They could all be potential customers, or they could have relatives and friends who could be potential customers.

For a while, some years ago, I spent time cold calling on companies - an experience I will never forget. I can still remember, and name, the companies who treated me well, and the ones who didn't! They certainly formed a lasting impression in my mind.

Here is a checklist to see if you are getting first impressions right.

First Impressions Checklist

Tick if you've got the following right:

❑   Is the entrance to your organisation clean and tidy?

❑   Is the name of the organisation prominently displayed?

❑   Have the logo and corporate colours been used on the signs?

❑   Are the doors clearly marked: 'Reception.'

❑   Are the company brochures on display? Are they up to date and fresh looking?

❑   Is the reception area clean, tidy and uncluttered?

❑   Is there somewhere for people to sit and wait in comfort?

- ❑ Is the receptionist dressed smartly or in a uniform provided?

- ❑ Does the receptionist smile on greeting the visitor?

- ❑ Does the receptionist get the visitor's name and use it?

- ❑ Does the receptionist invite the visitor to take a seat?

- ❑ Does the receptionist offer the visitor a tea or coffee?

- ❑ If there is a delay does the receptionist keep the visitor informed?

- ❑ Does the receptionist give good eye contact with the visitor?

When a staff member meets the visitor:

- ❑ Is the visitor greeted with a smile and the use of their name?

- ❑ Does the staff member shake hands with the visitor?

- ❑ Does the staff member open friendly conversation?

When the interview has finished:

- ❑ Does the staff member show the visitor out?

- ❑ Does the staff member shake hands, smile and thank them?

How is the telephone answered?

❏ Is the telephone answered within three rings at reception?

❏ If not what is the procedure if the telephone rings more than this?

❏ Is the telephone answered within three rings at the extension?

❏ Is the telephone extension answered with the staff member's name?

❏ Is there a message taking policy if the person is not available?

> **Remember: first impressions count.**

Take time to get all these vital elements right and do watch that reception area. When I train sales people I always tell them to get to the company they are visiting at least ten minutes before their appointment and sit in reception. There you can learn an awful lot about the company you are visiting, not only from the literature and what is displayed on the walls, but from the gossip. Unfortunately, or rather fortunately, for sales representatives, receptions are treated as social zones and everyone goes to them to gossip.

Once, whilst I was sitting in the reception area of a very large International company waiting to see the Commercial Director, two women did the most wonderful (or rather I should say awful) character assassination on the man I had yet to meet. I learnt a great deal about him, not all of it true, I'm sure!

There are other elements that go into communicating an image and here I have listed some of them.

○ **Your media coverage**
Is it favourable or unfavourable, or non existent?

○ **Sponsorship**
If you undertake sponsorship then how is your company name seen in the light of the sponsorship? Is it the right image?

○ **Brochures/leaflets/newsletters**
How is your name and company image portrayed on you marketing material?

○ **Advertising**
What image are you portraying through your advertising? Is it strong enough? Does it say what your company stands for? Do your staff advertisements communicate to potential recruits the image of your organisation?

○ **Stationery**
From your letterheads to your fax cover sheets what are you communicating to your customers? Is your letterhead too fussy or out of date? Are you using up old supplies of stationery with old logos and designs whilst at the same time using new stationery with new designs? If you are then your target markets are receiving mixed messages.

○ **Your staff**
What is the general attitude and appearance of your staff? Do they know what image your organisation

wishes to portray to its markets? If they don't how can they communicate this? Do they wear a uniform and if so what does this say about the organisation?

O **Your vehicles**
The appearance of your vans, cars, and lorries are important in communicating an image. If a van, or car, displaying your company name is badly driven then what does this say about your company? If the van or lorry is dirty and falling to pieces, what image is your organisation projecting? A pretty bad one, don't you think!

O **Signage**
If your company signage, both external and internal, is tatty, dirty or badly displayed, again it doesn't do much for image does it?

The Petty Matters Matter!

> **Take time to get all the things that go into making an image right and keep checking they are right.**

Building a competitive edge through price

Another and perhaps obvious way of building a competitive edge is through **price.** But it may not necessarily be the best way. You can be cheaper than the competition and so gain market share, but market share is not everything if sacrificed on the altar of profitability. Remember once your prices are low it is difficult to get them up again. In addition, you need to consider what image you wish to portray to your customers - cheap and cheerful, or value for money? It all depends on what market you are in and how your customers perceive you, the product or service, and its price.

Conversely you could charge a premium price and build a competitive edge this way. Perhaps you have an excellent image and reputation and this is taken into account when customers decide to buy from you. Price isn't everything and can often be of secondary consideration when quality and reputation are strong. I will look at pricing in more detail in the next chapter.

Product/service differentiation

You may have a product or a service that is very different to your competitors and therefore be able to gain a competitive edge. They say that imitation is the highest form of flattery and you can bet your bottom dollar that if you're doing something unique, or have a unique product, it won't remain unique for long. If it's good, imitators will come into your market, therefore, making product or service differentiation very hard to maintain.

Innovation is important. You should be constantly looking for new and better ways to deliver a service, or be searching for a better, more improved product.

Building and maintaining an excellent reputation

All the money you spend on marketing will be wasted if you don't get things right inside your organisation. If you have worked hard to win the customer and then things go wrong as soon as the customer buys from you, you might as well throw your money away.

Do good work and more work comes from it.

Having an excellent reputation in your field of expertise, or for your products, is the best way of building a competitive edge. But building a good reputation can take years of painstaking, hard work and only months, maybe even weeks, to destroy if you are not careful.

Building and maintaining a good reputation has to be worked at, constantly. No person, and no one organisation, can afford to be complacent. If you or your organisation become complacent then it is almost guaranteed that you will lose business and one of your most precious business assets; your good name.

Your staff are vital when it comes to maintaining a good reputation. In a service organisation at least 90% of the staff will come into direct contact with the customer. They may even deliver the service and as people buy people so your customers will be making buying decisions based on whether or not they like the people in your company. If they don't like them, they won't buy from them. In service organisations, marketing strategies and personnel strategies cannot be separated from each other. Therefore getting the right people and retaining them is absolutely vital.

And if you are marketing a product not a service aren't staff just as important? Of course fewer of the staff will come into direct contact with the customer but they all have a part to play in getting that product out of the factory gate on time and to the right standard. They rely on each other to do jobs efficiently and effectively.

If you have staff who couldn't care less, or who simply come in to work, do their bit, and then disappear as quickly as possible without being motivated by you, then their attitude will undoubtedly affect your competitive edge.

Do you remember that marketing orientation checklist in chapter one? Well, you want your staff working with you not against you and to do this they have to share the same vision as you. Your staff need to know what your organisation stands for, so define it and communicate it, consistently, not only through the written word but also through leading by example.

> **Define excellence and make it your objective.**

Ensure that excellence is led from the **TOP**. That means the business owner, director and manager. If it isn't it will fail.

Set standards of how you expect your staff to behave. And make sure you adhere to those standards yourself.

Ensure that if you have a dress and behaviour code that it is fair and consistent. You can't have one standard of behaviour and dress for your staff and a different standard for yourself or the management. When you draw up a behaviour or dress code make sure you involve your staff in this. These are usually highly contentious areas and can cause a great deal of friction. If staff are involved then they are more committed to making it work. Make sure you communicate these standards. Ensure that all your staff are clear on what is expected of them.

You will also need to examine training needs and issues like staff incentives. Give your staff a real sense of personal responsibility and try to develop an environment in which orders can be passed and carried out effectively.

Also give staff a sense of belonging - make them feel informed and involved. Ensure that they have a share in the success of the organisation. Happy staff make happy customers and therefore happy shareholders!

In order to ensure you have a well-motivated workforce you must be concerned with their personal wants, needs, and desires. There are no bad companies only bad managers. So you must make time to get staff relations right and continually work at it. It will pay dividends for the business if you have a happy, well-motivated workforce and it **will** contribute directly to the bottom line profit. Remember, I also said that you can get ideas for improving services or products from staff. So get their feedback and do this on a continuous basis.

Give your staff the training they need, not only for them to be able to do their jobs, but also in people handling skills. And plan for continuing training.

Make sure you measure and monitor performance. This can be done through regular and valued performance reviews or appraisals. Ensure that the staff members giving the appraisals are trained in how to do this and that the system is confidential and fair.

And don't forget to reward your staff. This does not necessarily mean a pay rise (although I am sure they would always welcome one!) but often a 'thank you' or 'well done' is enough. Too many of us are too ready to criticize and forget to give praise when it is deserved. People are motivated through praise, not punishment. Reward people through giving them extra responsibility or a different project. Training and development can also be motivating and rewarding.

Above all recruit the right people with the right attitude.

Action Points

1. Look at your own products. Have you developed a strong brand for them? Write down what that brand image is and then get your staff and customers to tell you what they think it is. Do you come up with the same points?

2. Conduct the first impressions checklists and identify areas that need to be put right. Make a list of them and say how you are going to put them right and when.

3. If you employ staff then carry out a staff audit. How happy and motivated are your staff? Examine their training needs and look at how you can improve the motivation of your staff.

Put in place a communications strategy to keep your staff informed and involved.

In summary

○ There are a number of ways you can build a competitive edge but the key to doing so and maintaining a competitive edge is consistency.

○ You can build a competitive edge through; branding, image, price, product or service differentiation and by having a reputation for excellence.

○ Branding is used to define identity and helps people relate to the product.

○ People will ask themselves if the brand fits with their lifestyle and identity, whether or not it is value for money.

○ Various factors go into making up a brand image. These include the product itself, the packaging, the advertising, the brand name, the price, how and where it is distributed and its availability.

○ Choosing a brand name can be tricky. The brand name should never contradict the essential product qualities. It should not have unfortunate connotations. It should be easy to say, pronounce, be catchy and should fit onto the packaging.

○ Having a clearly defined image for your business, products or services will greatly enhance your organisation's competitiveness and increase sales.

○ First impressions can be critical. Make sure they are the right impressions.

○ When building a competitive edge your staff are vital. Remember people buy people. Ensure that everyone is working for the organisation, not against it.

○ Building a good reputation for excellence in your field will ensure you get recommendations and repeat business.

○ Communication plays a key role in developing your staff to provide the desired corporate image.

○ Involve your staff, get their feedback and do this on a continuous basis.

○ Develop a personality for your organisation and lead it from the TOP.

○ Set standards for how you expect your staff to behave.

○ Give your staff the right training, not only for their jobs, but also in people skills.

○ Measure and monitor performance of your staff.

○ Reward your staff - remember to say 'well done' or 'thank you.'

Chapter five

Pricing

The prices for your goods or services will be set depending on a number of factors. For example:

O   your market

O   your product or service

O   your competitors

O   where your product/service is on the product lifecycle.

Pricing strategies will change. New entrants may come into your market, the attitudes of your customers can alter, technological breakthroughs will affect your product and therefore the cost of producing it and its positioning in the market place. You will need to constantly monitor your prices and adapt them accordingly.

So how do you set your prices? What pricing strategies are best for you?

Setting Prices

When looking at how you set your prices you need to consider the following:

O   Your business objectives - how much profit do you wish to make and over what period?

- ❍ Your costs for producing the product or delivering the service.

- ❍ The competition. How many competitors do you have? What are they providing and what is their pricing strategy?

- ❍ What is the demand for your products/services?

- ❍ Do you have a distribution channel mark up?

- ❍ What discounts, if any, are you offering?

When setting your prices you may have a variety of objectives. Here are some of them:

- ❍ To earn a target on investment.

- ❍ To maximise short or long term profit.

- ❍ To keep the business at a planned level of production, or to keep staff employed.

- ❍ To achieve a certain amount of growth in a required period.

- ❍ You may need to set a price that avoids government investigation and control.

- ❍ You set your price to enhance the image of the firm and its products or services.

- ❍ You set a price that will stabilise the market.

○   You set a price that will discourage entrants into the market.

○   To meet or follow the competition.

○   To stimulate cash recovery.

○   To be regarded as fair by customers.

○   To increase or maintain market share.

Obviously your business objectives can change and so too can the market. Your prices will change to reflect this.

There are a number of pricing strategies you can adopt. Many organisations use a variety of the ones I have listed.

Pricing Strategies

○   **Price Skimming**

Your product or service may be so different that it represents a drastic departure from the accepted ways of filling a demand or performing a service.

For example, when the Dyson Bagless Cleaner came onto the market it was the first of its kind. It could therefore be priced higher than other vacuum cleaners. It could skim or cream off the market before its price became more sensitive as other copycat products entered the market. The higher prices can also help to recoup some of the outlay on research and development.

O   **Market Penetration**

This is where low prices are used as an entering wedge to get into mass markets early. Direct Line Insurance used this pricing strategy when entering the market. They were unique in that they were the first to cut out the middle man (the broker) and sold insurance direct to the end user (the customer). They did not charge a premium price but went in cheaper than other competitors in order to gain market share. Strong potential competition is likely soon after the introduction of a new product or service when no 'elite' market, or no brand loyalty, exists and where people will respond to price.

O   **Competitive Pricing**

You will set your prices to meet that of the competition.

O   **Differential Pricing**

This is where you can charge different prices for the same product or service. This can be because of the different location of buyers, different types of customers or for large purchasers.

O   **Diversionary Pricing**

The actual price of the product or service is hidden in extras, i.e. installation, fitting etc..

O   **Dumping Price**

This is used to clean out excess obsolete stock.

A word about the Psychology of Pricing

Price can be taken as an indication of quality. If the price is perceived as being too high or too low then you may have to explain it or it will put people off.

I remember once, when I worked for Makro, the wholesalers, a range of office equipment was reduced to ridiculously low prices. There was absolutely nothing wrong with the equipment; it wasn't even obsolete but a genuine reduction. I watched as customers, initially attracted by the low prices, picked up the items and then put them down again. The goods were priced too cheaply. Customers thought there was something wrong with the products so they didn't buy.

People will also make a comparison between the product in terms of its 'perceived value,' i.e. is it seen as value for money.

Pricing can be linked to the packaging. Expensive packaging can associate the product in the eyes of the customers with expensive goods. Perfume is a good example of this.

Image can play another part in the pricing game. A piece of pottery or porcelain in a tatty junk shop priced low may not be bought because it is perceived to be rubbish. Clean it up and put the same piece in an expensive antique shop and the price can be trebled (unless of course you have knowledge of antiques and know its true value.) Image can be used to fool people or it can put people off. Is your price right for your company image and for the products it sells or the services it delivers?

When might you need to look at price changes?

You will need to consider price changes for any of the following:

○ **To help boost an ailing product.**

In chapter three we looked at the Product Life Cycle. When a product starts to decline you may decide to repackage it and relaunch it. If you do you may be able to raise the price. Alternatively, you may decide to lower the price of an ailing product to clear it out altogether. You may also be changing your prices by running 'special offers.'

○ **Loss leaders.**

This is a term more often associated with supermarkets. Sugar and bread are often used as loss leaders. They will draw the customer into the shop and once there the customer will make other purchases. You may decide to sell your product or service at a low price and not actually make any profit on it because you know it will lead to further business or more sales from that customer. Many solicitors use their Will writing service as a loss leader. Some even write Wills free of charge on the basis that once they write your Will you will return to buy your conveyancing, and other legal services. If the solicitor is good at cross selling this is often a very successful strategy.

○ **To counter the competition.**

You may decide to lower your prices to counteract the activity of the competition. You need to be careful here as any lowering of prices could lead to a downward spiral in the marketplace. Once down it is extremely difficult to raise your prices again.

You may decide to lower prices to win more work in a declining or stagnant market to help keep your workforce employed. The problems of lowering your prices could not only lead to a price cutting war, but it could also affect other products/ services in the range. It could change the customer's perceptions towards you and lead to an increased expense in promotion and an image of financial instability. For example, those shops which permanently have a sale!

Action Points

1. Examine your own pricing strategies, are they the correct ones?

2. What are your objectives and how will this affect your pricing strategy?

3. What is the image of your products/services and how are you perceived in the market place?

In summary

○ When you set your prices they won't stay the same forever. New entrants may come into your market, the attitudes of your customers can change, technological breakthroughs will affect your product and the cost of producing it and its positioning in the market place.

○ Price can be taken as an indication of quality.

○ People will also make a comparison between the product and its 'perceived value.'

○ Pricing can also be linked to the packaging.

○ You will consider price changes when launching a new product, to help boost an ailing product and as a loss leader to counter competition.

Chapter six

The market place and marketing planning

Part of your marketing involves you taking a look at your business and analysing its strengths and weaknesses. It also involves you looking at the market place in which your business operates and examining the opportunities and threats.

This is called carrying out a SWOT analysis. The SWOT analysis should be conducted at least twice yearly and your marketing plan should address the weaknesses in your business and build on the strengths you have identified. It should also state how you are going to capitalize on the opportunities and possibly what action you are going to take to overcome any threats to the business.

The strengths and weaknesses

What strengths does your organisation have that you can build on? What are the weaknesses that you need to correct? You may already have identified some strengths and weaknesses throughout the previous chapters.

For example:

Strengths

Good client base
Good product range
Clear vision of management
Well-motivated staff.

Weaknesses

Inadequate database
Weak on investing in new products
Web Site out of date or no Web Site
Reception area image poor
Recruitment problems.

The weaknesses will affect the performance of your organisation. Either eliminate them or turn them into strengths. Taking a realistic stock of your strengths and weaknesses is a must.

The opportunities and threats

What is happening in your market place now and possibly in the future that could affect your business? What action do you need to take as a result of this? The opportunities and threats are concerned with the external factors which affect your company and over which you have little or no control.

The same item could appear under both columns. For example, legislation introduced by the government could pose both a threat and an opportunity to your organisation.

The competition could also be both a threat and an opportunity - you may be able to take market share from your competitors and equally they could take market share from you.

Other things that need to be considered under these headings are:

O   **Consumer attitudes, changing lifestyles, habits, values and trends**

How will these affect your business? Identifying gaps in the market for new products and services could spring from being attuned to changing consumer patterns. Our lifestyle today is much faster than that of previous generations. Customers want their products delivered quicker, hence the growth of same day delivery services. Those organisations that spot the opportunities presented by changing consumer attitudes will continue to gain a competitive advantage and win market share.

O   **Technological developments**

How will technology impact on your business? One of the most radical changes in recent years has been the introduction of the personal computer, the microchip and of course the Internet. Digital television is set to open up new markets and change buying habits. E commerce is a reality. Can your organisation embrace it and exploit it as an opportunity to reach new markets or are your competitors leaving you behind? How will technology change the way your business operates? How will it change the way your customers choose a supplier or buy goods?

O   **Legislation - both UK and EU legislation**

What new legislation is on the cards that could affect the operation and profitability of your business? This can involve not only UK legislation but also European legislation. Perhaps new legislation will open up a new market for you? Perhaps it will seriously affect the viability of your business.

O   **Economic**

Recession, recovery, interest rate increases or decreases. How much money do people or businesses have to spend or invest? How will this affect your company's performance?

You will also need to monitor the changes taking place around you with regard to suppliers. Changes in their market may well affect you. New channels of distribution are opening up with the World Wide Web, others may be closing down. How are you responding to these changes?

You need to be aware of what is happening in your own market and the wider – macro - environment. Looking ahead and being prepared is half the battle. Adapt your marketing accordingly to meet these opportunities and threats.

The Marketing Planning Process

What I have done in the previous chapters is take you through what is called the marketing planning process. I have posed the questions you need to answer in order to market your business more effectively. Let's just sum up the marketing planning process so far.

Step 1. Identify your target markets

Divide your existing and potential customers into easily
identifiable groups. Understand who your customers are,
where they are, what they buy, why they buy, how much
and when. What value do they put on your products or
services? What markets are you really in?

Step 2. Identify your services/products

What is the range of products or services on offer? Is this
the right mix for your target customers? Where are your
products or services in relation to the Product Life Cycle?
Are they in the introduction, growth, maturity or decline
phase? What are the features and benefits of the products/
services you offer?

Step 3. Identify your competitors

Where are you in the market place in relation to your
competitors? What are your competitors' strengths and
weaknesses? What is your brand share, market share? What
are your competitors' prices, sales strategies? What new
products or services are they developing?

Step 4. Identify your competitive edge

Carry out an Image audit. Just what is the image of your
business? Carry out a staff skills and performance audit - do
you have the right staff with the right level of skills? Carry
out a customer satisfaction audit - are you delivering what
your customers want? Identify how you are going to build
your competitive edge. Is this through:

O People

O Service or product excellence

O Reputation

O Image

O Price

O Or all the above.

Step 5. Carry out a SWOT Analysis

Identify the strengths and weaknesses within your organisation. Say what you are going to do to build on the strengths and eliminate the weaknesses. Identify the external opportunities and threats.

Now we need to look at setting the Marketing Objectives.

Setting Marketing Objectives

Most Marketing Plans run for a year at a time but it is a good idea to set, or at least have some idea of, your broad objectives in the longer term; say three to five years. A word of caution though, it is becoming increasingly difficult to plan very far ahead as the pace of change today is so fast and the introduction of new technology is daily re writing the text books on business operation and business development. Having said that, however, you still need to set objectives at least on an annual basis.

When setting your objectives it is not enough to say that

you want to be the best company in town - how are you going to measure that? How do you know when you are the best?

Your objectives therefore have to be specific and measurable. In short they need to be **S.M.A.R.T.**

S.M.A.R.T. stands for

Specific
Measurable
Achievable
Realistic
Timed

Here are some examples of objectives that meet the above criteria.

O   To increase market share of x product/service from 10% to 20% of the current market by January 2001.

O   To increase sales of x product/service from £1.8m to £2m by January 2001.

O   To maintain % profitability levels on x product range over the year.

O   To investigate at least two new markets and to identify one key market to penetrate in 2001.

Whatever your objectives ensure they are realistic and achievable. I often find that when I go into companies the owners or directors have set themselves too many objectives that they can't possibly hope to achieve. This is demotivating. So don't be too ambitious.

Marketing Strategies

So how are you going to achieve your marketing objectives? How are you going to increase sales, increase your customer base, build profitability etc.?

There are four basic marketing strategies to help you. These are:

1. Market Penetration

This involves keeping your existing customers and finding new ones.

2. Product or Service Development

This involves improving your existing products or services i.e. improving the quality, adapting the style, offering something new etc. for your existing customers.

3. Market Extension

This involves finding new markets for your existing products or services i.e. going further afield geographically or appealing to a new group or type of customers.

4. Diversification

This involves increasing your sales by developing new products for new markets.

This final strategy carries the highest cost and the highest risk. You are entering a market you know nothing about, with a product or service you have no experience of. Usually, businesses adopt a combination of the first three strategies to achieve their objectives.

Following this you need to develop a marketing action plan for each strategy to help you achieve your objectives. You may have a marketing action plan for each target group of customers and/or for each product or service supplied. The next chapter looks at the promotional tools you can use in your marketing action plan to help you achieve your objectives.

Action Points

1. Carry out a strengths and weaknesses analysis. These are concerned with the internal aspects of your business. State the action you will take to correct the weaknesses. Your marketing plan should also state how you are going to build on your strengths.

2. Carry out an opportunities and threats analysis. Remember these are concerned with factors outside your control in the external market. Identify any opportunities. Your marketing plan should state how you are going to exploit these opportunities. Identify the threats and say what you can do to minimise these?

3. Set your objectives for the next year at least or review the ones you have already set. Are these S.M.A.R.T.?

4. Identify the marketing strategies you are going to use to help you achieve your objectives.

In summary

○ A SWOT analysis should be conducted twice yearly. This looks at the internal strengths and weaknesses of your business and the external opportunities and threats.

○ Marketing objectives should be S.M.A.R.T. This stands for:
> Specific
> Measurable
> Achievable
> Realistic
> Timed.

○ Don't set too many objectives. If you can't fulfill them you will become demotivated.

○ There are four basic marketing strategies to help you achieve your objectives. These are:
> Market Penetration
> Product/Service Development
> Market Extension
> Diversification.

○ Usually businesses adopt a combination of the first t hree strategies to achieve their objectives.

○ You need to develop a marketing action plan to help you achieve your objectives.

Chapter seven

The Marketing Action Plan

So, having answered all the questions in the preceding chapters you are now ready to look at how you are going to target your customers and potential customers.

You will have identified whom you are targeting, with what products or services and why your customers buy these products and services.

You will also have identified what it is they are buying: the benefits of those products and services. You will have an understanding of your target markets so that you are able to talk the language of customers in those markets.

You will have a clear brand identity, or identities, for your products and services and a clear image for your company and your products/services.

You will also have reviewed your prices and set these.

You will know what your strengths and weaknesses are and will be building on these strengths and taking action to eliminate, or minimise, the weaknesses. You will be planning how to capitalise on the opportunities you have identified and you will be aware of the threats to your business.

You will have set your marketing objectives and identified which marketing strategies are the most appropriate for you.

There may be other issues you need to address - internal issues - like staffing. You may need to refine your database, or start working on developing new products or services. You may be surveying your customers to find out what their level of satisfaction is with your products or services, or looking at developing a Web Site or E commerce.

Having gained a clear direction of where you are heading and whom you are targeting, you need to identify the right promotional tools to reach those target customers.

> **People can't buy from you unless
> they know you exist.**

So you need to communicate with them. You need to tell them you're there!

There are a number of ways you can do this and a number of promotional tools you can use. You have to decide what tools, or what mix of tools, are the best. This will depend on:

O   what you are hoping to achieve i.e. your objectives

O   what budget you have set

O   whether or not it is the appropriate method for that particular group of customers.

This chapter lists some of the promotional tools. The next chapter gives you some tips on how to use them.

Some of the promotional tools

○ **Advertising**
television
radio
newspapers
magazines
directories
wall planners, diaries etc.
poster advertising e.g. hoardings, railway platforms,
bus shelters, buses etc.

○ **Signage**
business premises
cars, vans etc.

○ **Promotional items**
notepads
pens
carrier bags
t-shirts etc.

○ **Direct Marketing**
mail order catalogues
off-the-page advertising
direct response advertising
mailshot letters
mailshot leaflets
door drop leaflets
inserts into magazines
telemarketing
the Internet.

○ **Editorial**
press releases and articles

○ **Taking a stand at exhibitions and trade fairs**

○ **Personal Selling**
having a sales representative on the road and calling on prospects.

○ **Seminars/Demonstrations/Open Days**
inviting your prospects and customers to a seminar, demonstration and open day.

○ **Corporate Hospitality**
inviting prospects and customers to a corporate hospitality event. Your satisfied customers should help you sell to your prospective customers.

○ **Sponsorship**
initiating your own sponsorship deal, or going in on the back of existing ones, like theatre sponsorship. You can tie this element in with editorial coverage and corporate hospitality.

○ **Sales Promotion Techniques**
merchandising - making sure your product is displayed to the maximum effect.
giving special offers e.g. two for the price of one, discounts, 10% extra etc.
joint promotions - tying up with someone else.

○ **Personal Recommendations**

Much of your business should be generated through existing customers who come back to you and buy more from you, or who recommend you to others. Getting it right inside the organisation - your internal marketing - is extremely important. Chapter four looked at this in detail.

You may be able to think of other promotional tools you can use to target your customers.

Questions to ask before using any of the promotional tools

Before you decide to use any of the promotional tools you should stop and ask the following questions:

1. What is my objective?

Be clear about what you are trying to achieve from the outset. For example, you may be advertising to stimulate sales and prompt enquiries. Alternatively, you may be advertising with the purpose of raising name awareness only amongst your target audience. This is a very different objective that will not directly stimulate enquiries in the short term, but could benefit you long term, especially if carried out consistently and in conjunction with other promotional tools.

You may be holding a seminar to increase your organisation's profile in its target market. Enquiries may not come in at the seminar itself but later, when you follow up the contacts made with a direct mail letter, telemarketing call, brochure and even possibly a special offer.

You may be carrying out a direct mail campaign with the objective of increasing your database. Once you have names on your database you can then begin to communicate with these prospects on a regular basis, perhaps through telemarketing them, inviting them to a seminar or exhibition, sending them special promotions and of course keeping in touch with them on a regular basis through your newsletter.

You may be attending an exhibition, not with the primary purpose of getting orders or leads, but because if you're not there your competitors and the visitors may think you've gone out of business or that you're in financial difficulties!

These are just some examples. The main message is to know what it is you are hoping to achieve then you will be able to measure the success of it. And, of course, you must always track results.

2. Can my message be creatively different and is it the right message?

How are you going to communicate your message through this promotional tool? Don't forget you must communicate the benefits of what you are offering, in the language that the target market understands and can relate to.

You must also look at the image you are portraying, and brand values if appropriate. How are these being communicated with regard to the promotional tool you are using?

You will need to think about your target customers and how they will react to the message. How do you wish them to react? Define this and check back that you are achieving it.

3. Will using these promotional tools reach my target audience?

Have you chosen the right promotional tool to reach the right target audience? Remember back to chapter two when we looked at what markets we are in. Always ask yourself whether or not this promotional activity will reach your target market.

4. How am I going to follow this through?

The key to successful marketing is consistency - consistently putting out the right message to the right target audience. People buy what they are familiar with, so you need to keep your company name, and/or your products or services, in front of your target customers on a regular basis. It is not enough to advertise once and then say, 'well that didn't work onto the next thing!' You will need to build awareness for your products or services over a period of time, through a campaign, this could be by advertising, using direct marketing or through the press.

Why businesses fail in their marketing is mainly down to three things:

O   they don't understand what markets they are really in and therefore try and be everything to all people;

O   they don't understand why their customers buy from them and therefore don't communicate the right messages;

O   they flit from promotional tool to promotional tool not giving any of them time enough to work.

Make sure this doesn't happen to you. Draw up a programme of marketing activity. It doesn't have to be grandiose or extravagant, simply producing a half yearly newsletter and a press release once a month may be enough. In fact, it may be all you can afford and need. Sending a mailshot quarterly and following up with telemarketing and/or a sales visit may be the right approach for you. A small advertisement in the right magazine once a month may work, and you may combine this with a mailshot to certain target customers. Or attendance at one or two key exhibitions, with leads being conscientiously followed up with mailshots and telemarketing could get you results.

> **So identify who you are targeting, with what message and how over the next year.**

Write it down. Say when you are going to do it and stick to it, even if you are frantically busy because it is when you are busy you should be marketing. Another classic mistake is to take your foot off the gas when the going is good. When sales dry up further down the line you are then coming from too far behind for your marketing to take effect immediately.

Action Points

1. Look at the markets you are targeting. What promotional methods are you going to use to reach them and communicate with them? Are they the right promotional tools?

2. What is your objective in that target market - will that promotional tool achieve that objective?

3. Write down who you are going to target and say how. Put beside it who will be taking the action and how much it is going to cost you.

In summary

❍ There are a number of promotional tools you can use. You have to decide which tools, or which mix of tools, are the most appropriate.

❍ You will need to consider what you are hoping to achieve, what your budget is and whether or not it is the most appropriate method for that particular group of customers.

❍ Before you decide to use any promotional tools you should ask - can demand for this product/service be stimulated by using this promotional tool?

❍ You can't measure the success of the promotional tool unless you know what it is you wish to achieve in the first instance.

❍ Always track results.

❍ You must communicate the benefits of what you are offering, in the language that the target market understands and can relate to.

❍ You must also communicate your image and /or the brand values if appropriate.

❍ Be consistent in your approach. People buy what they are familiar with, so you will need to make them aware of your company and its products or services over a period of time.

Chapter eight

Tips on using the Promotional Tools

In this chapter I will examine some of the more popular promotional tools and provide you with some golden rules and tips that will help you to use them more effectively.

Advertising

Advertising can often be the most costly and the least effective of the promotional tools, particularly when it comes to the smaller business working on a low budget. Of course it can bring you results but be clear about why you are advertising and what you hope to achieve by advertising. You will also need to make sure you are advertising in the right medium to attract your target audience.

Advertising must create a sense of familiarity as I have already mentioned in the previous chapter. People buy what they know and recognise. Advertisements over a period of time therefore build familiarity, raise awareness and credibility. One off advertisements rarely achieve anything. So when you are considering advertising you almost certainly need to look at a campaign. This builds your company name and awareness in the mind of your target audience. Your advertisements should also create an image that is compatible with the product/service and your organisation.

Advertising Objectives

When you consider running an advertising campaign you need to think of your objective i.e. what it is you are trying to achieve. Here are some objectives:

O   to build demand for your product or service on launch,

O   to give the customer details and instructions on how to use a product,

O   to build brand recognition for your product,

O   to create a certain image for the brand, or for the company,

O   to give information about a price promotion and so stimulate demand,

O   to build names and addresses on the database,

O   to educate people - e.g. drink driving campaigns, no smoking campaigns,

O   to back up sales drives,

O   to influence consumers to buy.

Before you advertise you will also need to know the answers to those questions I posed in chapters two and three, namely:

O   who buys your product or service?

❍ why do they buy it?

❍ what is it used for?

❍ what is the extent of advertising needed to reach that target group of customers?

❍ how much do you need to do to get the message across?

You also need to answer the following questions:

❍ What media are my target customers exposed to?

❍ What do I know about the media?

If it is a printed publication then obtain a copy of it. See who else is advertising in it and try telephoning a couple of the advertisers to ask about their response.

What is the content of the editorial and would it appeal to your target customers? Ask yourself if they would buy and read this magazine or newspaper. Ask the publication what their circulation and readership figures are, and what profile of customers the publication is aimed at. If you are considering radio or television then ask who listens to the radio station, or who watches that programme?

How often is the magazine/newspaper/directory etc. published? What are the rates, the copy deadlines and what special deals will they do for you?

Ensure that the media details match with your target audience. Then, if having satisfied all the above, you decide to advertise, how can you make your advertising more effective?

In order to work adverts must be:

Seen
Read
Remembered
Believed
Acted upon.

Firstly then, you have to get the advertisement seen or heard i.e. it must appear in the correct media, or on the correct radio or television station, at the right bus stops and railway platforms etc..

Next the advertisement has to be read. What makes you look at an advertisement? How many times have you looked up at a hoarding whilst sitting at the traffic lights and have read what is on the board in front of you? Have you remembered it? Have you gone to turn the page of a magazine or newspaper and found yourself instead reading and responding to an advertisement? It worked. Ask yourself what made it work?

Some golden rules for using promotional tools

The following is the golden rule for many of the promotional tools, whether it is designing an advertisement, writing a mailshot letter or leaflet, or writing for an insert or brochure.

You need to grab their ATTENTION.

You only have a couple of seconds before someone turns the page and misses your advertisement. You have a couple of seconds before they put your mailshot letter in the waste paper bin, or lift the insert from the magazine and throw it away. So you need to make sure that you grab their attention.

To do this you need to be imaginative. Try using a strong headline or a bold question that captures or plays on your key benefit. Remember back to our features and benefits exercise in chapter three? It is the benefits that persuade people to buy, not the features.

On television, obviously you can use a number of techniques to capture the imagination.

Television and Cinema are moving pictures with sound and vision both of which you can exploit, but that doesn't necessarily mean people will keep watching, they may zap channels, or pop out to make a drink, or buy an ice cream, therefore missing your expensive advertisement.

Again, you need to think of your target audience and capture their imagination perhaps through humour, a story line, a cartoon or nostalgia.

Sound will make people notice your advertisement on the radio. You can use sound effects, a good voice artist or music to get the attention.

In the printed media, which most of us will be concerned with, you can use colour to make your advertisement stand out in a mainly black and white publication. Or you could use a black or coloured border. Borders are very effective. Illustrations or photographs also work well. Or you could use a combination of the above. But **don't** fall into the trap of trying to cram too much text into too small a space.

Use white space to help your advertisement stand out.

Keep it simple. Too much text and your advertisement will be lost in all the other text on the page.

Look through the advertisements in magazines and newspapers to see which ones stand out. Ask yourself why and then adapt the technique to suit your own advertisements.

In **a mailshot letter, leaflet or flyer**, essentially you are writing advertising copy. So again you need to put your key benefit first or pose a question to get the reader's attention.

Don't begin a mailshot letter with waffle, or with the standard, 'I am writing to introduce my company to you.' It's obvious you are writing and besides I didn't invite you to introduce your company to me did I? And if I read another letter starting with, 'In today's competitive climate,' I think I will scream. I know it's competitive so please don't tell me what I already know!

If you don't make your letter easy to read then why should your reader bother with it? You haven't got time to wade through lots of text searching for the benefits so don't insult your reader by thinking that they are not as busy as you are.

Once the mailshot letter, leaflet, flyer or advertisement has caught the recipient's attention what you hope is that the reader, watcher or listener will stay reading, listening or watching! To do this you need to:

Stimulate INTEREST.

Here, we return once again, to our features and benefits exercise. What are the other benefits you are offering? Make these benefits strong in your advertising copy, mailshot letter and leaflet, to add conviction.

When writing the copy always remember your target audience, what language do they speak? What will they respond to?

In a mailshot letter use short words, short sentences and short paragraphs. Use YOU and I instead of WE. Remember you are trying to create the impression of writing to them personally so make it user friendly. Use frequent sub headings or bullet points to break up copy. Be clear, straightforward, uncluttered and avoid jargon. Be as natural as you can, as if you are having a conversation with the person.

Always consider the reader's needs, in your advertisement, leaflet, flyer or letter. Make sure you interest him/her by giving benefits.

Remember people always ask 'what's in it for me!' Address this question in your advertisements, mailshots. Tell them what's in it for them.

Develop interest with the best benefit and win them over with second and further benefits. Follow your copy through from the heading. You must get the reader saying, 'Yes, I must have some of that!' And there must be something in the letter, leaflet or advertisement for the reader wherever he/she looks. Make it easy for the reader or listener to understand what the offer is. They shouldn't have to spend hours fathoming it out, and of course they won't.

Having gained interest you then need to:

> ## Inspire DESIRE.

Strengthen your benefits. You can use questions to hold the interest and build desire.

Be enthusiastic. Be friendly. Be helpful. Again revisit your features and benefits. Add in the features that would appeal to the target customers emphasising the benefits, for example free car parking, a free quotation, money back guarantee, an accessible location, friendly helpful expert staff, long and convenient opening hours, or an easy way of ordering.

Make your target customers really want what you are offering.

> ## Finally prompt ACTION.

Tell the customer what he or she should do now i.e. call us. Make the telephone number bold or add in a coupon or a fax back. Let them tick boxes; people find it easier and quicker.

Give an incentive for them to take action, use a free trial, free consultation, free brochure and free gift possibly.

> ## So remember A.I.D.A.
>
> ## Attention – Interest – Desire - Action

Some extra words
on promoting a service

Promoting a service is not easy because a service is intangible - you cannot demonstrate it, touch it, taste it etc. So how do you communicate your message? And how do you differentiate what you are offering to that of your competitors?

The rule of **A.I.D.A.** also applies here but, in addition, you need to capture the personality of the service organisation - what it stands for. You need to try and build a strong image through your advertising, and an image that people will remember.

In service advertising you need to get the reader to identify with the company. This can be done through consistently promoting the right image. We looked at image in chapter four.

Direct Marketing

If used correctly Direct Marketing can be a very effective way of marketing and winning new business.

Direct Marketing provides the opportunity for your potential customers to buy direct from you without using a third party i.e. you can reach your customers direct.

Direct mail in particular can be phased and targeted and the response monitored. It is an excellent marketing tool for both large and small businesses alike.

What areas does Direct Marketing cover?

❏   'Off the Page'

These advertisements appear in many colour supplements and magazines. Customers can buy the product 'off the page' paying by cheque or credit card, either by using the coupon response or by telephoning to place their order.

❏   Direct Response Advertising

This is where your products can be sold direct through advertising. Charities cost effectively raise thousands of pounds through their direct response advertising campaigns targeted at key times throughout the year, like Christmas. People will telephone the number given and give money via their credit card. Many other products and services, like Insurance for example, are sold through advertising direct on the television and radio.

❏   Mail Order Catalogues

There has been a rapid rise in the number of excellent products being sold through mail order catalogues. Boden, Racing Green, The Art Room, The Cotswold Company and many more specialist and general catalogues exist today. Viking Direct sells stationery direct through catalogues and many other consumer goods and business-to-business products are sold in this way. Can you put your products into a catalogue and sell through mail order?

❑ **The Internet**

Like mail order there has been a considerable increase in the number of people using the Internet to buy products. Many companies promote their services on the Internet. Predictions are that the Internet is set to change the way we buy forever. It will get quicker to use and therefore it will be easier to shop in this way. Again, can you use the Internet to sell your products and/or to promote your services?

❑ **Telemarketing**

My book, *'The Easy Step by Step Guide to Telemarketing, Cold Calling and Appointment Making'* explains this area in much greater detail. Telemarketing can apply to both inbound and outbound calls and again, with the advent of technology, we have seen a rapid growth in this area. The telephone as a marketing tool can be used successfully by large and small businesses alike.

It can be used:

○ to help you build and maintain relationships with your existing customers, to get them to buy more from you

○ to answer queries and deal with customer complaints

○ to carry out market research

○ to sell to new customers.

❏   **Direct Mailings**

This includes:

○   mailshot letters

○   leaflets

○   door drops

○   inserts.

Well targeted and well designed mailshots, in particular, can be an extremely successful form of marketing. They are controllable and the results can be measured. We have already looked at the golden rules for writing mailshot letters and leaflets, but there are some additional rules you'd do well to remember to ensure your mailings don't become junk mail.

Secrets of a Good Mailshot

○   **The Mailing List**

This must be as accurate as possible and up to date. The mailshot must be targeted to the right person and must be sent to a named individual.

○   **The product/service and the offer**

There must be something in the mailshot for the reader. A strong offer and clear benefits.

○   **The sender must have an affinity with the receiver**

You must communicate the right message. Again you need to look back to the work we've already done in chapters two and three. In order to be successful you must talk the language of your target customers.

O **A response mechanism**

You must make it easy for the reader to respond. Give them a coupon to complete and post, or a fax back. Or make your telephone number bold to encourage them to pick up the phone to you. Freepost and a Free Phone number can help to lift response.

Newsletters can be effective mailshots

Newsletters are an effective marketing tool in that they can keep both your existing customers and target customers informed of new products and services. They also help to keep your company name in front of your customers.

Newsletters can help to build rapport with your existing customers and gain loyalty from them. By keeping your organisation's name in front of your prospects it will help to stimulate sales and enquiries.

But in order to work Newsletters must be produced regularly. This can be quarterly, three times a year, or simply twice yearly. Produced regularly your customers and prospects will come to expect them and they will also come to rely on receiving them. Newsletters should also contain valuable information for the customer and should certainly not just be company sales puff.

Corporate Brochures

Do you need a corporate brochure? What are you going to do with it when you get it? I have been to many organisations where the corporate brochure has cost them the earth and yet it sits collecting dust in the bottom of a cabinet. I have even had people say to me that their brochure is too expensive for them to send out - what was the point of producing it then!!

You must ask what is the purpose of your brochure. Is it to be mailed to people on request? Is it to be displayed in reception? To be taken to an exhibition or for use by the sales force? Or are you going to use it for all of these things and more.

Who is it aimed at? What target audience are you trying to communicate with? If you have a wide cross section of target audiences do you need several brochures to communicate with them?

What special, unique selling points or benefits are you going to emphasise in your brochure? What image are you trying to portray? What is the personality of your company and how can this be communicated in your brochure? Does the brochure need photographs or illustrations? Should it be full colour, one colour or two? What size should it be? All these questions need to be answered and to do that you need to know how you are going to use the brochure and who you are targeting.

In addition, never have too many people involved in the design of a corporate brochure or it will end up looking as though a committee has designed it. The essential message and image will have been diluted, or even lost completely. Remember it is not what you would like in a brochure but what your target audience would like.

And, of course, look at your budget. Corporate brochures can be expensive. Make sure you spend your money wisely on a brochure that serves its purpose and that it will work for you and reach the right target audience.

Exhibitions

Before agreeing to undertake an exhibition you should ask yourself why you are exhibiting. What do you hope to achieve from it? Here are some objectives for exhibiting:

O   To meet existing customers and improve your relationship with them.

O   To meet potential customers, identify new opportunities and prepare the ground for future sales.

O   To promote your organisation and its image.

O   To inform customers and potential customers of new services/products or changes.

O   To obtain sales leads.

O   To prove you are still in business!

Questions to ask for Exhibiting?

Before exhibiting ask yourself the following:

O   **Is it the right Exhibition for my business?**

Are your customers and potential customers going to be there? Who will attend the Exhibition?

O   **How are the organisers promoting the Exhibition?**

Are they going to do enough to attract visitors?

O   **What will it cost? You need to consider the following:**

Cost of the space
Cost of hiring or producing a stand
Cost of material
Cost of your time
Cost of any lost business whilst you are away.

O   **Design of your stand**

Who is responsible for this? What image do you wish to create? The stand should be welcoming and accessible. Corner stands are ideal as access is available from three directions. Alternatively a stand sited at the bottom of a stairwell can prove to be a good location.

Make sure you have the right literature and don't display it too neatly otherwise visitors will be afraid of disturbing your work of art.

It is also a good idea to have something moving on display, a piece of equipment, a computer programme, or a video. If played loudly it attracts visitors to your stand. But make sure it doesn't run on endlessly. Stop and start it at loud places especially when visitors to your stand are flagging.

Make sure you have enough staff manning your stand. You should always have at least two people on the stand for the majority of time. Exhibition work is very tiring and people do need to take a break, have a coffee and go to the toilet. In addition, if you have at least two people, you can have a pre-arranged signal between you to get rid of the time wasters.

After the Exhibition

Many organisations fail to track the results of an exhibition. This seems crazy when you think of the amount of money they cost. You must evaluate the success or otherwise of undertaking that exhibition and you must be prepared to track contacts for some time afterwards; months, years even. Look at:

○   How many leads did you get?
○   How many orders did you get?
○   Ask if the exhibition was worth attending and would you do it again.
○   How much did it cost you - was this recovered with orders received?

Ruthlessly follow up all contacts made, and keep in touch with them. Use mailshots and newsletters to do so. Invite them to an open day or seminar.

Sponsorship

If you decide to undertake sponsorship, or initiate one yourself, you must ask yourself why you are doing it and what you hope to achieve through it.

Some objectives for Sponsorship could be:

○ To enhance the image or reputation of your company.

○ To build links in the community.

○ To reach a new target audience.

○ To promote your company name and image.

Define who you are aiming at - what sort of people? How will they see your company name and in what connection will it be associated? Then ask if this is the right image?

How much will you have to pay for the sponsorship and what does this cover? What can you get out of it, for example, extra press coverage, entertaining at an event? Also consider these extra costs.

Are there any other sponsors and if so who are they? Are they your competitors? Also ask how long the sponsorship lasts for.

Building a Positive Press Profile

Editorial coverage is an extremely effective way of raising your company profile. Editorial carries at least two and half times the weight of advertising. People believe what they read in the newspapers. If the newspaper says you're an 'expert' then you become an 'expert.'

What can press coverage do for your organisation?

Press coverage can:

○ raise your organisation's visibility and credibility with customers and prospective customers

○ stimulate sales of goods and services

○ set you apart from the competition

○ help to motivate employees – everyone likes to work for a successful organisation

○ help to attract good quality recruits

○ help to reinforce the other messages you are sending out.

> **The secret to successful press coverage is in pitching the right story to the right media at the right time to convey the right message to your target audience.**

So what are your possible news stories?

There are many 'news' stories to tell within an organisation. Here are examples of just some of them:

○ winning new orders
○ retirements
○ new appointments
○ promotions
○ new products or services
○ celebrations, like anniversaries
○ winning awards
○ success of trainees

O involvement in local charities

O good financial results.

Scan the local and national newspapers to see what makes the news. Look at your trade or professional magazines to see who is hitting the headlines and with what kind of story. Develop a journalistic eye and look for the angle - the element that makes the story appealing and different. The list of possible stories is endless. Set yourself targets for writing and distributing at least one press release a month.

Press release layout guide

O Use 'News Release' headed paper preferably with your company name on.

O Type neatly with double spacing and wide margins and use only one side of paper.

O Don't underline anything and if you go onto a second page put 'more....' at the bottom of the first page.

O Don't split a sentence between one page and the next. Staple the pages together and get someone to proof read it for mistakes before it goes out.

O Send it first class post, or e mail it if the newspaper or magazine accepts e mail. Wherever possible address to the journalist by name.

Writing Your News Release

The news release is written in a certain style. Here are some tips to help you write yours.

○ The headline must encapsulate the story - what the release is about. Don't try to be a tabloid headline writer because the editor or sub editor will use his or her own headline anyway. Your headline is used purely to capture the journalist's attention.

○ The first paragraph is the key to the release. It must contain the whole story, the angle and your organisation's name, where you are based and what you do.

○ The second paragraph goes on to give the details already summarised in paragraph one. The facts and figures if necessary. You may only need one paragraph of explanation otherwise two will probably be sufficient.

○ The third paragraph is the quote and the fourth paragraph may contain more practical facts. If the release is about a new publication or event it can give a contact name and telephone number.

○ The final sheet carries **ENDS**, and the date. Then, **'For further information contact'** and give details of contacts within your company for the journalist or editor.

In summary

O   Advertising can often be the most costly and the least effective of marketing tools, so you should use it wisely.

O   You will need to make sure you are advertising in the right medium to attract your target audience.

O   Advertisements over a period of time build familiarity and raise awareness and credibility. One off advertisements rarely achieve anything.

O   Before you advertise you need to know who buys your product/service and why they buy it?

O   Remember A.I.D.A. Attention – Interest – Desire – Action.

O   As with all your communication tools think benefits not features.

O   If used correctly Direct Marketing can be a very effective way of marketing and winning new business.

O   Direct Marketing provides the opportunity for your potential customers to buy direct from you without using a third party.

O   Direct mail in particular can be phased and targeted and the response monitored. It is an excellent marketing tool for both large and small businesses alike.

○ The mailing list must be as accurate as possible and up to date.

○ The mailshot must be targeted to the right person and must be sent to a named individual.

○ There must be something in the mailshot for the reader. A strong offer, clear benefits.

○ You must communicate the right message - talk the language of your target customers.

○ You must make it easy for the reader to respond.

○ Newsletters can keep both your existing customers and target customers informed of new products and services.

○ Newsletters can help to build rapport with your existing customers and gain loyalty from them.

○ By keeping your organisation's name in front of your prospects it will help to stimulate sales and enquiries.

○ If designing a corporate brochure ask who it is aimed at. Remember different people talk different languages; perhaps you should have a series of brochures to serve different markets.

○ What unique selling points or benefits are you going to emphasize in your brochure?

○ What image are you trying to portray? What is the personality of your company and how can this be communicated?

○ Before agreeing to undertake an exhibition you should ask why you are exhibiting. What do you hope to achieve?

○ Make sure you have enough staff manning your stand. Do look welcoming and talk to people. Open the conversation gently.

○ Ruthlessly follow up all contacts made. Use mailshots and newsletters. Invite prospects to an open day or seminar. Keep in touch with them.

○ Decide why you are undertaking sponsorship and what you hope to achieve by it?

○ Press coverage is an extremely effective way of raising your organisation's profile.

○ The secret to successful press coverage is in pitching the right story to the right media at the right time to convey the right message to your target audience.

○ There are many 'news' stories to tell within an organisation. Scan the local and national newspapers to see what makes the news.

○ Look at your trade or professional magazines to see who is hitting the headlines and with what kind of story.

○ Develop a journalistic eye and look for the angle - the element that makes the story appealing and different.

○ Set yourself targets for writing and distributing at least one press release a month.

○ Keep releases short. One page, or one and a half pages, double-spaced.

○ Make sure your timing is right. Don't send out a release for something that happened months or weeks ago.

○ Think up creative angles for your stories and use creative photographs.

○ Use 'News Release' headed paper preferably with your company name on.

○ The first paragraph is the key to the release. It must contain the whole story, the angle and your organisation's name, where based and what you do.

Chapter nine

Putting it together – Your Marketing Plan

Quite often businesses don't undertake any of the groundwork we have done in this book. We didn't even look at promotional tools until chapter seven! So don't leap in with a promotional tool until you have thought it through. Don't be reactive but proactive.

You will need a mix of different promotional marketing tools to achieve your objective, which ultimately must be to win new business. Chose and use them wisely.

You need to consistently communicate with your target audience in the way they understand.

You need to consistently look at the products and services you deliver and ensure these are what your customers want.

You need to consistently look at your organisation and the market place in which it operates.

And most of all don't forget those existing customers. Existing customers are the easiest customers to sell to. They buy more from you and they can recommend you to others. Make sure you get the internal aspects of your marketing right. After all it's no good spending money on external marketing - the promotional tools - to find that once you've brought the customer in something goes wrong inside the organisation and you lose them.

If you employ staff then make sure they are working for you, not against you. You want staff motivated and loyal, taking a pride in delivering to the customer. Re read the chapter that looks at the internal marketing of your organisation. The staff, the image, first impressions are all important. Return to that marketing orientated questionnaire in chapter one and make sure you can tick yes to all the questions. What do you have to do to keep your customers coming back for more? Do it now and keep doing it.

Finally, I have laid out for you on the following pages a summary of marketing action points. If you answer these action points you should end up with a marketing plan for your business that, I sincerely hope, will bring you every success.

Action Point 1.

Take a look at your organisation and the services or products it produces; are these what the customer wants?

Do you tap into your customers' comments about your products or services? Have you asked your customers what they want?

Start now - telephone a sample of customers or devise a questionnaire to capture their comments after a transaction.

Gain feedback from your staff if they regularly interface with your customers. Do this exercise regularly and analyse the results.

Action Point 2.

Look at your own customer base and analyse who is buying from you?

O   What sort of people are they? What type of businesses?

O   Where do they come from?

O   How much do they spend?

O   Which are the most profitable sectors?

Start capturing this information on a database and analyse it on a regular basis.

Action Point 3.

Draw up a list of features for your business, and for each product or service you provide. Then say to yourself, "so what? - What does this feature mean to the customer?"

Put the benefit to the customer along side that feature.

Are these benefits promoted strongly in your marketing literature? If they aren't re write your literature and incorporate the benefits.

Action Point 4.

Look at the volume of sales generated for each product or service.

Compare this with previous years' performance, then plot

your range of products and services on a life cycle.

Which products/services would you say are in the maturity or growth phase? Which in decline?

Have you any new products/services being developed or introduced? Should you be looking at this?

What are you going to do to start this process and when are you going to do it?

Action Point 5.

Have you developed a strong brand for your products?

What does that brand mean to you, to your staff, to your customers. Have you asked them? If you all come up with the same or similar words when talking about your products or services, then you are branding, and successfully. If there is a difference, or people can't say what your products represent, then you are failing.

Do your customers and target customers know what your brand image is? Do you? State it now. List the characteristics of your products/services.

Action Point 6.

Carry out an Image audit on your business. Identify those elements that are giving out a favourable image and those that are giving out an unfavourable image. What are you going to do to turn the unfavourable images into favourable ones?

Conduct the first impressions checklists and identify areas that need to be put right. Make a list of them and say how and when you are going to put them right.

Action Point 7.

Carry out a staff audit. How satisfied are your staff? Do you motivate and train them? Do they know what your organisation stands for?

Examine your recruitment policies. Have you identified what sort of staff you require? Do you induct them, inform and involve them?

Action Point 8.

Examine your pricing strategies.

Are these the correct ones?

Action Point 9.

Carry out a strengths and weaknesses analysis. These are concerned with the internal aspects of your business. List them and identify action to correct the weaknesses. Say how you are going to build on your strengths?

Carry out an opportunities and threats analysis. These are concerned with factors outside your control in the external market. Identify any opportunities for your organisation. Say how you are going to exploit these? Also identify the threats - what can you do to minimise these?

Identify your competitors

○   Who are they?

○   What are they selling/providing and how?

○   How can you be better or different to them?

○   How/what do you need to change?

Action Point 10.

Set your objectives for the next year. Make sure these are S.M.A.R.T. i.e.

> Specific
> Measurable
> Achievable
> Realistic
> Timed.

Identify the marketing strategies you are going to use to help you achieve your objectives.

> Market Penetration
> Product/Service Development
> Market Extension
> Diversification.

Action Point 11.

For each group of target customers and/or each product or service say what promotional tools you are going to use over the next year to target them and what results you expect.

Focus in on who your customers are, both actual and potential. Identify growth areas. State what action and what promotional tools you are going to use to target them. Put beside this when you are going to use them, who is responsible for seeing that they happen and how much it will cost you.

Action Point 12.

Set your budgets and say when you are going to review your plan.

The Marketing Plan Summary

1. Marketing Objectives

State these. They should be:
> specific
> measurable
> attainable
> realistic
> timed.

2. Current Situation Analysis

Give a summary of your:
> strengths
> weaknesses
> opportunities
> threats.

This section should also include information on:
> your competitors
> your target markets
> your key products/services
> your staff capabilities
> your image
> your competitive edge.

3. Marketing Strategy

Identify the key strategies your company is going to take to meet its objectives.

4 Marketing Action

Try and break this down by target market sectors, giving marketing action for each sector as appropriate.

Identify the promotional tools needed to target these market segments. These could include:

>   Advertising
>   Direct Marketing Campaigns
>   Exhibitions
>   Publicity
>   Sponsorship
>   Sales Promotion
>   Personal Selling
>   Telemarketing
>   Existing customer relations/cross selling
>   initiatives.

5. Set your budget

Cost the above promotional tools and add your budget into your plan. Identify a budget for the development of any new products/services.

6. Review

Build in a timetable for reviewing the plan and make sure it happens. Take corrective action if you are not meeting your objectives.

Remember: Focus: Target: Act: Review: Adapt

Good Luck!

www.rowmark.co.uk